Stories for the Lord's Supper

Communion meditations from everyday life

Douglas Redford

STANDARD
PUBLISHING

Edited by Theresa C. Hayes
Cover design by Robin Moro

Library of Congress Cataloging-in-Publication Data

Redford, Doug
    Stories for the Lord's Supper / Doug Redford.
        p.   cm.
    ISBN 0-7847-0945-9
    1. Communion sermons. 2. Story sermons.
3. Sermons, American. I. Title.
BV4257.5.R39   1999
252'.6--dc21   99-12644
                                     CIP

06   05   04   03   02   01   00   99   5   4   3   2   1

USING THIS BOOK

Jesus often began instructing his followers by telling a story. As we examine his words we will hear him say, "In a certain town . . ." or "There was a man who . . ." or even "Suppose one of you . . .".

The meditations in this book begin with simple stories—in most cases, the stories of experiences to which almost everyone will relate. After bringing hearers together on this *common* ground, speaker and listener can move together to *higher* ground, the authority of Scripture.

This book can be used in a number of ways. You might simply refer to the author and read the meditation as it is written. Another approach is for the speaker to change the first-person references (I, me, we) to third-person references (he, him, us) when using the devotion. But may we encourage another strategy?

In the margin of each meditation is a suggested way to "**Make it your own.**" We recommend that you personalize the meditation by sharing an experience *of your own* similar to that of the author. Since these stories relate incidents common to us all, this is usually an easy task.

The telling of simple stories has been used to effectively communicate complex truths for centuries. May you find this method helpful when you tell these **Stories for the Lord's Supper.**

CONTENTS

To William and Katherine Redford—
my parents,

whose godly example
helped to shape the course
of my walk with God.

A CHILD'S PORTION

MATTHEW 18:1-4

In the fall of 1997, we purchased a home. During the process of moving into what became my study, I noticed some markings on the door jamb. Upon closer examination, I discovered that the markings had names by them; the previous owners were keeping a growth chart for different members of the family. And it wasn't just for the children— one of the higher marks had "Grandpa" written beside it.

Children enjoy reaching certain milestones that indicate they are growing or getting taller. At the amusement park they take delight in riding a certain ride that they were not allowed to last year, because now they are taller than the height line that separates those who can ride from those who aren't permitted. When they reach a certain age, they get to order from the grown-ups' menu instead of having to choose from the kids' meals.

The meal provided at the Lord's Supper is a meal that no one ever gets too old or too mature to need. We never reach a stage of maturity that allows us to say, "Oh, I outgrew that a long time ago—I can afford to skip it every now and then."

No matter how long we have been Christians, we must all come before this table as children of the heavenly Father. There is no pecking order, by which those who have been Christians the longest get to be served first or get the biggest share to eat. The fact is that we are all unworthy to be present at such a table as this. That someone has been a Christian for many years does not increase his worthiness; he is still a sinner saved by grace.

Perhaps it's a good thing that we take a small piece of bread and a small amount of juice when we take the Lord's Supper, for these are children's portions, are they not? And that's exactly how we must always come to this table—as little children.

Make it Your Own

Do you know a story that illustrates the excitement of a child reaching a milestone—getting to do something or go somewhere that was off limits previously? Tell that story at the beginning of this meditation.

DATE USED _____

AT THE KING'S TABLE

2 SAMUEL 9:6-13

During my junior year in college, I served as one of the class officers. Among the junior class's annual duties was the planning of the Junior-Senior Banquet. Our responsibilities included finding a good location, securing a speaker, doing proper publicity, and selling tickets.

When our group began to consider suggestions for a speaker, we decided to be ambitious. We targeted a nationally known personality whose Christian convictions we believed would provide a powerful challenge to us and would make our class's banquet one of the most unforgettable ever. There was one problem, and it was a big one—*cost*. The figure that our proposed speaker wanted was far beyond what we could afford. It was going to be impossible to bring him to the banquet (without saddling the banquet fund with about a twenty-five-year debt—a legacy our class did not want to leave behind).

Most of us can only dream of what it would be like to have dinner with—or just meet—a well-known personality or public figure. But think of the privilege that is ours at this time of Communion each Lord's Day:

we are given a place at a King's table—the King of kings! These emblems remind us that we are not here because we have the resources to be here; we are here in spite of our woeful lack of resources. We are here, not because of what we've done, but in spite of what we've done. The only way we could ever afford to be where we are now is if someone offered to pay the admission price. That is what Jesus—the King himself—did at the cross.

Make it Your Own

Can you think of a special event you would like to attend or a person you would like to meet—yet the chances of doing so are slim because of the cost? Tell that story to begin this talk. Or perhaps you were privileged to meet someone famous. Tell about what a special occasion that was.

Our position is similar to that of Saul's grandson, Mephibosheth, who marveled that he could be treated like one of King David's sons and be given a place at the table of the king. In fact, in the short narrative describing David's kindness to Mephibosheth, his place at the king's table is mentioned four times (2 Samuel 9:7, 10, 11, 13). Such was not the common way for a king in the ancient Near East to deal with the relatives of his predecessor; he usually did away with them in order to assert his authority.

If Mephibosheth was overwhelmed by such treatment, how much more should we be on this occasion as we gather before our King's table?

DATE USED _____

10

Baby Talk

Because my wife and I both have younger siblings (she has two younger sisters and I have a younger brother), our children have had the opportunity to see some of their younger cousins grow from infancy and master such milestones as walking and talking. Our eighteen-year-old daughter was playing with one of her cousins (about a year old at the time) and listened her to plead, "Ba-ba!" Thinking she wanted a ball, our daughter scrambled to find one that would suffice. It wasn't until a few minutes had passed that she realized that her cousin wanted a bottle, not a ball. Such are the challenges of deciphering baby talk.

Of course, this cousin, God willing, all too quickly will form very clear syllables, words, phrases, and sentences. She will not need to ask others to get objects for her; she will soon seem far too independent for her own good. She will move beyond a bottle to a variety of other foods. And all too soon will come the day when she celebrates her eighteenth birthday, leaving us to wonder where the time went.

The Bible speaks of becoming a Christian as a rebirth, or as being born again (John

3:3). The writer of Hebrews encouraged the Christians in his day to grow in their faith and to move on from milk to solid food. Indeed, he seemed frustrated at their lack of progress in doing so (Hebrews 5:11-14). It is not that all Christians must be at the same level of growth or maturity; however, all Christians *must* keep making progress—going forward from milk to solid food, then learning how to handle the solid food.

Yet when we come to this meal at the Lord's table, the menu always features the same items: the bread and the fruit of the vine. And it doesn't matter whether you've been a Christian for six days or sixty years—you take the same portion at this table. Why? Because no matter how mature you are in Christ or how long you've been a Christian, you are still dependent on Jesus' death to save you. Every one of us has to come to God by way of the cross. This table will not let us forget that.

Make it Your Own

Do you know a story that illustrates how hard it can be to communicate with a baby—or a story that tells something humorous about a baby? Use it to begin this meditation.

DATE USED _____

BIG BROTHER

HEBREWS 2:10, 11

Our two sons, Jon and Tim, were born approximately four and a half years apart. When we phoned to tell Jon that he had a little brother, he turned to the friend he was staying with and they said to each other, "All right!"

Over the years, our boys have developed a close friendship and have shared a lot of common interests. Part of this closeness can be attributed to the fact that they shared a room. When we moved into a larger house, each of the boys was able to have his own room—a move that was long overdue, since at that point Jon was 15 and Tim was 10.

It was quite interesting, however, to observe what happened. Though each boy had claimed he couldn't wait until he had his own room, it wasn't more than a couple of days until they started spending time together in each other's room! Even today, though Jon is driving and is a bit more independent, he continues to enjoy being a big brother—and Tim enjoys having one.

Whenever we come to this Communion table, there are a variety of ways to consider what Jesus means to us: he is Savior,

Redeemer, Deliverer, Messiah, Lord. One of the titles that may not be quite as familiar is Elder Brother—a designation that is explained by Hebrews 2:11: "Both the one who makes men holy and those who are made holy are of the same family. So Jesus is not ashamed to call them brothers." We are all in the same family because God "has given us new birth into a living hope" (1 Peter 1:3) and thus the privilege of being able to know him as our Father.

Think of what it means to have a big brother like Jesus. This big brother is not ashamed of us, as Hebrews 2:11 says. He never wants us to get lost. He never has more important things to do than listen to us. He always stands up for us and is always available to give us his counsel on how to handle the world and its pressures. After all, he's been there, done that (Hebrews 2:18; 4:15).

It's too bad that George Orwell gave the phrase "big brother is watching you" such a negative connotation in his book *1984*. The fact that our big brother—Jesus—is watching out for us is one of the greatest comforts we can have.

DATE USED _____

Make it Your Own

Do you have a personal illustration to tell about having or being a big brother? If this does not apply to you personally, do you know of another family where it did or does? Use such a story to begin this talk.

BLOOD GIVEN, BLOOD TAKEN

JOHN 10:17, 18

From time to time, my wife gives blood at a local hospital. That process is a careful, deliberate procedure. The hospital makes an appointment for her to come, and usually they call her a couple of days or so ahead of time just to remind her of the date. (If she has been ill, they advise her to postpone her visit until she is fully recovered.)

When she arrives at the hospital, she has to fill out a lengthy questionnaire designed to determine whether or not her blood is acceptable. Then a technician checks her temperature, blood pressure, and iron level. Only after she has passed all these tests can her blood be taken.

This is an entirely different scenario from that of the criminal who stabs or shoots his victim and produces blood. In that case blood is shed, but it is certainly not given.

We think of how Jesus was so cruelly and brutally treated by his enemies. They fastened him to a cross by driving nails in his hands and feet. They made his blood flow. When he breathed his last, it appeared that they had taken his life.

Yet in all of this, Jesus was fulfilling a plan. His life was not being taken; he was *giving* his life, *giving* his blood. Peter declared, "This man was handed over to you by God's set purpose and foreknowledge" (Acts 2:23). Jesus himself stated, "The reason my Father loves me is that I lay down my life—only to take it up again. No one takes it from me, but I lay it down of my own accord" (John 10:17, 18).

People give their blood to save others from physical death. Jesus gave his blood to save us from spiritual death. Unlike those who must make repeated appointments to give blood, Jesus had only one appointment to keep—and he kept it without fail.

Today we are gathered before this table not to remember someone whose life was tragically taken from him but someone who gave his life and offered his blood because he loved us.

Make it Your Own

Have you ever given blood? Or do you know a story about giving blood? Use that one with this meditation.

DATE USED _____

16

BRIDGING THE GAP

During the summer of 1997, our daughter participated in a short-term mission trip to Nicaragua. Among the items that she was to bring were pieces of hard candy and small toys or trinkets. These were to serve as ice-breakers for the Nicaraguan children. Most of them lived in deprived conditions and did not get many treats or toys. The hope was that these gifts would open a door that would lead to friendships that would pro-duce opportunities for a Christian witness to both the children and their families.

Such actions as these helped to bridge an existing gap between two different cultures. They could well be placed in the category of becoming "all things to all men [or in this case, 'all children']" with the aim of winning some (1 Corinthians 9:22).

We usually think of the Great Commission as the portion of Scripture where Jesus tells us to "go into all the world and preach the good news to all creation" (Mark 16:15). But the truly Great Commission occurred when Jesus left the glory of Heaven and came to this world to rescue lost mankind. Sometimes a missionary is thought of as someone who ventures into a foreign field.

You can't get any more foreign than traveling from Heaven to earth!

The emblems we are about to take remind us of the enormous gap that Jesus bridged when, as Philippians 2:7 tells us, he "made himself nothing, taking the very nature of a servant, being made in human likeness." That likeness is remembered through the meaning of these emblems. To think that "the Word was God" (John 1:1) and that "the Word became flesh" (John 1:14) is the most compelling illustration of Paul's becoming "all things to all men" principle. Someday we will bridge the gap between earth and Heaven when Jesus returns and we rise to "be with the Lord forever" (1 Thessalonians 4:17). That hope is also conveyed through these emblems, since we are to partake of them "until he comes" (1 Corinthians 11:26).

Jesus was not just born; he was sent. He came to us to fulfill his Father's commission. His death was no accident. It was part of the Father's plan—and now we are part of that plan. Jesus said so: "As the Father has sent me, I am sending you" (John 20:21).

Make it Your Own

Do you have a story of how you bridged a gap in communicating spiritual truth (or any message) with a child, a person from another country or culture, or anyone whose differences forced you to think of creative ways to get your message across? Use that story here.

DATE USED _____

18

CROSS-EXAMINATION

Some time ago I received one of those letters that you know is bound to come someday, yet you wince when it arrives. It was time for me to fulfill my civic responsibility and report to the courthouse for possible jury duty. And so that is where I drove on the assigned morning.

When all the potential jurors were present, the clerk informed us of the procedure to follow. One of the steps was called *voir dire* (vwahr <u>deer</u>)—a French phrase meaning, "to speak truly." In this process, the potential jurors are questioned by the attorneys representing the parties in the case being tried. The attorneys use this examination to determine who they would like to place on the jury (in other words, who they might be more apt to persuade with their arguments). After the *voir dire* is completed, the attorneys meet with the presiding judge and select those individuals who will comprise the jury.

A similar process of *voir dire* occurs whenever we meet to take the Lord's Supper. This investigation is not conducted by a preacher, an elder, a Sunday school teacher, or any group representing the church. Paul

19

instructs us, "A man ought to examine himself before he eats of the bread and drinks of the cup" (1 Corinthians 11:28). This is a personal time of examination; however, that is not to say that we set the standards for judgment. If we set the standards, the judgment likely would be too lenient. In fact, as Paul observes in verse 31, "If we judged ourselves, we would not come under judgment." We might not speak truly.

But Paul continues in verse 32: "When we are judged by the Lord, we are being disciplined so that we will not be condemned with the world." Whereas the attorneys were concerned with how a person's background, occupation, education, and other factors might affect his or her perspective on the case being tried, the Lord is concerned with how our perspective of faith has affected these factors. Am I his person between Sundays?

This table is meant to make us think. It is meant to make us face some tough questions about ourselves. But better that we ask these questions of ourselves now than to hear the Lord ask them of us at Judgment Day.

DATE USED _____

Make it Your Own

Have you ever served on a jury or gone through the process described above? Tell about your experience (perhaps mentioning a specific question that you had to answer) at the beginning of this talk.

20

DON'T GET TOO CLOSE!

HEBREWS 10:19-22

Our three children always have shown an interest in helping my wife and me with certain tasks around the house (though the enthusiasm of the older two has waned somewhat since they entered the teenage years). One of the jobs that our two boys have found particularly fascinating is starting the fire on the grill whenever we cook outdoors. Knowing the dangers that can accompany unsupervised curiosity, I've been very careful to guide them slowly through the procedure. When the time comes to strike the match and ignite the coals, I tell them, "As soon as the match catches fire, throw it on the coals and move back right away. *Don't get too close!*"

The system of worship under the Old Covenant was a carefully structured one. Certain parts of the tabernacle (later the temple) were meant only for certain designated individuals. The most restricted area was the Holy of Holies, which only the high priest could enter—and that only once a year on the Day of Atonement, to offer an atonement for the sins of Israel. When Jesus died, the Scripture says that the veil (curtain) of the temple (marking the entrance into the Holy of Holies) was torn completely from top to bottom (Matthew 27:51). This signified an act that was clearly God's doing, not man's.

No visual aid could have provided a more compelling testimony to the impact of Jesus' death on man's relationship with God. The Old Covenant system, with its numerous barriers and limitations, had declared to the Israelites, "Don't get too close!" In contrast, as Hebrews 10:22 tells us, the message of the New Covenant is "Let us draw near to God. . . ." The barriers are down! The limitations have expired! Don't stay away any more!

The Lord's Supper is a time for us to reflect on the glory of this unlimited access to the Father. It isn't offered to only a select group of Christians. Everyone who has named the name of Jesus as Lord has the opportunity and the privilege to remember him at this table.

Let us *all* draw near.

Make it Your Own

Tell about a time when you had to stay away (or told someone to stay away) from something especially harmful.

DATE USED _____

God's Plus Sign

Matthew 16:25; John 10:10

Signs of one kind or another greet us every day. Some are the normal variety that we see while driving (and sometimes ignore at our own risk), such as "Speed Limit," "No Parking," "School Zone," and "Exit." Other signs grab our attention because they break the norm; they say something that signs always have said, only in an unconventional (and usually humorous) way. I once drove by a home where a realtor, instead of placing a "Sold!" sign in the yard, had posted one that read, "Too late!"

Whenever our family goes back to the small town where we used to live, we all watch for the sign indicating that we have arrived. All travelers have their own special signs to watch for, such as the golden arches of McDonald's (for the kids) or "Rest Stop" (for the driver!).

Most church buildings display a cross at a prominent place in the sanctuary—usually somewhere up front where all the worshipers can see it. A little boy who came to church for the very first time (and had no idea what church was all about) noticed the cross at the front of the sanctuary. He nudged the person who had brought him and asked, "How come they have a plus sign on the wall up there?"

That little boy didn't understand the cross very well—or did he? The cross is the clearest, most vivid sign there is that God loves us. He wants us to stop running and come home. He wants to take our lives out of the minus column and put them in the plus column. He wants to add all that was subtracted when man fell in the garden of Eden. He wants to forgive us of all the negatives—all the can'ts, didn'ts, and shouldn'ts—that have made life empty and give us a life "to the full" (John 10:10).

Some believe that being a Christian is a losing proposition—that you don't get back as much as you give up. To them the cross is a minus sign, not a plus sign. That is directly opposed to what Jesus said: "Whoever wants to save his life will lose it, but whoever loses his life for me will find it" (Matthew 16:25).

So the little boy was right. In a world filled with negatives, put-downs, criticism, and finger-pointing, the cross remains God's plus sign to us.

Make it Your Own

Do you know a story about a particular sign (a road sign, a billboard, etc.) that was or is significant for a certain reason? Use that story to begin this meditation.

DATE USED _____

24

Good as New

It has happened more than once in our family. On one of the most recent occasions, we bought our younger son a plastic basketball rim—the kind you can hook over the top of the door so that you can close the door and play basketball in your room (great for cold, rainy days). He had played with it only a few hours when (perhaps as the result of an overly enthusiastic slam dunk) one side of the rim snapped in two. Neither taping nor gluing would help; the rim was broken.

It's hard for children to understand how something new can get broken so quickly—and hard for parents to explain to a crying child! But brokenness is a part of life; we cannot escape it. We grow from the disappointment of broken toys to the frustration of faulty cars, washing machines, and vacuum cleaners.

In the spiritual realm, brokenness is a much more positive quality. Vance Havner once wrote:

> God uses broken things. Broken soil to produce a crop, broken clouds to give rain, broken grain to give bread, broken bread to give strength. It is

25

the broken alabaster box that gives forth perfume. It is Peter, weeping bitterly, who returns to greater power than ever. (*Leadership*, Winter 1983.)

Consider the emblems of the Communion table. Here is bread, made from broken grains of wheat, representing the body of Jesus broken for us. Here is juice, made from broken or crushed grapes, representing the blood that was given when Jesus' body was broken.

These symbols remind us that the only way we can come to Christ is to come *broken*—for only then do we understand why Jesus came and did what he did. He did not come to commend whole people; there were none. He came to fix broken people—the only kind there were (and still are).

God could have discarded us as rejects, too damaged by sin to be of any further use. Instead, he chose to fix us—to remake us. That is why Jesus, who didn't need to be fixed at all, was broken for us at the cross. He was broken that we could be restored, forgiven, and made good as new.

Make it Your Own

Can you think of an example of something (like a child's toy) that broke or failed to work properly not long after it was purchased or given as a gift? Use that story at the beginning of this talk.

DATE USED _____

Good Timing

Some of us remember watching (or listening to, during the radio days) Jack Benny—one of the most popular comedians of our time. One of the reasons he was so funny was his impeccable sense of timing. He knew just when to speak, when to pause, and how long to pause so that the audience could laugh at what he had said or done. When he died in 1972, Bob Hope said, "Here's one occasion when Jack's timing was off—he left us too soon."

Some would look at the life and death of Jesus, and say, "He died too soon. He was tragically killed in the prime of life—if only he could have lived longer, how much more he could have done." But Jesus' timing was not off; it was perfect. He came in "the fulness of the time" (Galatians 4:4, *King James Version*), and he died in the fullness of time. Hear Peter's words from Acts 2:23: "This man was handed over to you by God's set purpose and foreknowledge."

Jesus' death was tragic, but it was no accident. His death did not catch God by surprise. God was not left wringing his hands, crying, "They've killed my Son; now what will I do?"

Consider these words from Max Lucado's book, *The Cross:*

The journey to the cross didn't begin in Galilee. It didn't begin in Nazareth. It did not even begin in Bethlehem. The journey to the cross began long before. As the echo of the crunching of the fruit was still sounding in the garden, Jesus was leaving for Calvary. . . .

And when human hands fastened the divine hands to a cross with spikes, it was not the soldiers who held the hands of Jesus steady. It was God who held them steady. Those same hands that formed the oceans and built the mountains. Those same hands that designed the dawn and crafted each cloud. Those same hands that blueprinted one incredible plan for you and me.

Take a stroll out to the hill. Out to Calvary. Out to the cross where, with holy blood, the hand that placed you on the planet wrote the promise, "God would give up on his only Son before he'd give up on you."

(Multnomah Publishers, 1998, pp. 23, 24)

Make it Your Own

Do you have a story that illustrates the importance of good timing (perhaps from the world of sports or music)? Use that story in place of the Jack Benny story.

DATE USED _____

HOME IMPROVEMENT

JOHN 14:23

When we were purchasing the house in which we now live, we were told to have an inspection done. Then, if any problems surfaced, we could negotiate with the seller about addressing them before we agreed to buy the house. It is a practical application of the oft-quoted maxim, *Caveat emptor* (<u>cav</u>-ee-aht <u>emp</u>-tor), which means, "let the buyer beware."

For the most part, the inspection went well. It was conducted by a group called, appropriately enough, the "Home Team." The team did turn up some minor problems that we were able to take care of with little difficulty. Some other repairs were suggested, but were not considered serious enough to stand in the way of our purchase.

Inspections—they're highly recommended for condos, cars, and Christians. At the Communion table we subject ourselves to a period of inspection, or more accurately, *introspection*, where we inspect (or examine) ourselves (1 Corinthians 11:28). To think of this inspection in terms of a home is not at all off the mark. Jesus once said, "If anyone loves me, he will obey my teaching. My Father will love him, and we will come to him and make our home with him" (John 14:23). The presence of the Holy Spirit (whom someone once described not as the Holy Ghost but as the Holy Guest) signifies the presence of "Christ in you, the hope of glory" (Colossians 1:27). Each Christian is to become a place where God's Spirit feels more and more at home.

Communion gives each of us the opportunity to conduct an inspection of his or her house and to ask some pointed but necessary questions. Are there certain rooms in my house to which I still hold the key? Have I been keeping my foundation solid, or have I allowed it to shift and weaken? Does the roof protect me from harmful elements on the outside that would clash with Christ's presence? Are there leaks that need to be fixed before they cause serious damage? Are the windows clean, giving me a clear view of the world of hurting, aching people—the "sheep without a shepherd"—whom Christ calls me to serve? Does Jesus really have the title to this house—*all* of it?

If we want to spend eternity in Jesus' house, we need to make sure that he is welcomed in our house.

Make it Your Own

Have you ever gone through the process of having a house inspected? Was something unusual or unexpected found? Or do you know of someone else's inspection that turned up something interesting? Use such a story to begin this meditation.

DATE USED _____

30

Keep It Simple

My father was a man of simple pleasures and simple tastes. It did not take a lot to make him contented. Among his favorite pastimes was batting balls in the front yard to my younger brother and me. When he was hot and thirsty after working outdoors, nothing satisfied him more than a tall glass of ice water.

The pace of life for me is so much faster than it was when Dad was my age. The challenges I face with my children are so much more complex than those Dad faced with me and my brother and sister. Tough as it may be to accomplish, I hope that I can maintain the same love for simple things in my life that Dad possessed.

When Jesus gave us a way to remember the meaning of his death for us, he did not provide a lengthy theological treatise. He did not preach a sermon or teach a lesson, then give a pop quiz to see if the disciples were listening. His actions and his words were deliberately simple: he took bread, blessed it, and told the disciples to eat of it. Then he did the same with the fruit of the vine. And that is all that Paul, according to 1 Corinthians 11:23-26, related in his description of Jesus' institution of the Lord's Supper. That is the simplicity that the Corinthian church, with all its jealousy, infighting, and carnality, had lost.

Roberto Goizueta was chief executive officer of Coca-Cola for a number of years. He once said in an interview, "This is a very simple business. When we complicate it we really mess things up" (*Wall Street Journal*, October 20, 1997, B1). When you come to this table each Lord's Day, you will see what you see today: bread and juice. The simplicity here should keep us sensitive to the simplicity of the gospel: "Christ died for our sins . . . was buried, . . . [and] was raised on the third day" (1 Corinthians 15:3, 4).

In a world of complexities and confusion, this table reminds us to keep our message and our mission simple. When we complicate it, we really mess things up.

Make it Your Own

Do you know of someone who exemplifies simplicity or who loved simple pleasures? Use that person's story to begin this meditation.

DATE USED _____

KEEPING APPOINTMENTS

HEBREWS 10:25

Driving my family to the train terminal in Fort Wayne, Indiana, one evening, my wife and I realized that we were going to have to step on it to get to the terminal before the train left. We had never made the trip before and hadn't allowed ourselves enough time. When we arrived, I hardly had time to kiss my wife good-bye! I was reminded of those times during my school years when I would happen to miss the bus home and had to call my mother to come and get me.

As we grow older and begin accepting additional responsibilities, we learn the importance of keeping appointments. Being late for a job interview or missing a day of work because of oversleeping is much more serious than missing the school bus. And most people can't call for parents to come and get them out of their predicament!

The appointment we have chosen to keep this morning—being present at the Lord's table on the Lord's Day—is one that needs to receive top priority every week. It seems that even in New Testament times, getting Christians to maintain consistency in corporate worship was a challenge. Too many had become lax in keeping their appointment.

That is why the writer of Hebrews had to tell them, "Let us not give up meeting together, as some are in the habit of doing" (10:24). A bad habit indeed!

The writer goes on to say, "Let us encourage one another—and all the more as you see the Day approaching." I would suggest that the "Day approaching" refers to the return of Jesus—the "blessed hope" of every Christian (Titus 2:13). That day *really* will be the Lord's Day! How do we prepare for it? By taking this Lord's Day seriously. We prepare for the assembly on that day by being faithful to the assembly on this day. We prepare for the great supper to be served at the wedding of the Lamb (Revelation 19:9) by the faithful observance of the Supper set before us now and offered each Lord's Day.

Never forget that, no matter what the week to come may bring, this is the most important appointment you will keep this week. Treat it as such.

Make it Your Own

Do you know a story that illustrates the importance of keeping an appointment or the cost of missing an appointment? Tell that story with this meditation.

DATE USED _____

LET THERE BE LIGHT!

2 CORINTHIANS 4:6

Some months ago, during a typical summer storm, the lights in our home went out. When it became apparent that the lights were not just flickering but were off to stay, our youngest son became excited. "This will really be cool," he said. But it didn't take long for the coolness to wear off. Not more than fifteen minutes later, he was complaining, "I'm bored. Isn't there anything to do?" Darkness was not quite as much fun as it first appeared.

When Adam and Eve sinned against God in the garden of Eden, a spiritual power outage occurred. They did not experience the positive results that the serpent promised. Instead, a terrible darkness engulfed the world. Yes, the sun continued to shine; the moon was visible at night; the stars came out at their appointed time. But spiritually, something tragic had happened—something that the best attempts of men were powerless to reverse.

Then, as the writer of a well-known gospel song put it, "One day when sin was as black as could be, Jesus came forth to be born of a virgin!" The world notes Jesus' impact in history by dating events as B.C.

35

and A.D. We could also mark his birth by observing that the world took a dramatic turn from P.M. to A.M.—from darkness to light. The prophet Isaiah foretold Jesus' impact in these words: "The people walking in darkness have seen a great light; on those living in the land of the shadow of death a light has dawned" (Isaiah 9:2).

With Jesus' coming the spiritual power outage ended; both the darkness and the prince of darkness were dealt a mortal blow. Paul writes in 2 Corinthians 4:6, "For God, who said, 'Let light shine out of darkness,' made his light shine in our hearts to give us the light of the knowledge of the glory of God in the face of Christ." We live in the era of God's re-creation—his second declaration of "Let there be light!"

As we come to this table today, let us give thanks that the "true light" (John 1:9) has come to dispel the most frightening, oppressive darkness there is—the darkness of sin. Rest assured that whenever the storms of life gather strength and threaten us, this light will never go out.

Make it Your Own

Can you tell of a time when the lights went out— in your home or your work, or on a particular occasion that proved embarrassing or difficult to deal with? Use that story to begin this meditation.

DATE USED _____

LOST AND FOUND

LUKE 15:22-24

Plymouth, Indiana, is the home of the Blueberry Festival—a three-day extravaganza that lasts through the Labor Day weekend. The festival attracts huge crowds every year. Food and craft booths pack the local park, and the weekend is filled with activities to suit a wide variety of interests. The small, normally laid-back town of Plymouth is transformed into a hub of activity.

Given the throngs of people at the festival, sooner or later some little ones are bound to be separated from their families. Those children are taken to the information center to wait while an announcement is made over the loudspeaker for the lost parents to come and get their child. You can't help but feel sorry for such a little one, who is usually in tears by the time Mom or Dad reach him.

Lost. It can be a disturbing, alarming word, especially when children are involved—and not only small children, but big ones, too, like the young man in Jesus' parable of the prodigal son. As many have observed, it is perhaps more descriptive of this parable to call it the parable of the loving father. In his joy at seeing that his lost son has returned home, the father has the fattened calf butchered and prepares a feast. How good that must have tasted to the young man after surviving on pig pods!

Here at this table each Lord's Day we take the meal that commemorates our homecoming to the Father. We recognize that our Father did much more than kill a fattened calf for us; he gave his only Son as the spotless Lamb to be a sacrifice for our sins. Each of us gathered here as once lost but now found can picture our Father saying these words (inserting his or her name in the proper place): "For _____ was dead and is alive again; _____ was lost and is found."

Of course, we do not want to dwell on the past; we want to "press on toward the goal" (Philippians 3:14). But it may be helpful from time to time for each of us to ask, "What direction would my life have taken if I had never come home to the Father? Where would I be without Jesus?" The answer is really very simple: *lost.*

Make it Your Own

Do you know a story about a person or an object that was lost but then eventually was found? Tell that story at the beginning of this talk.

DATE USED _____

MORE THAN SPECTATORS

EXODUS 32:26

Many of us remember Richard Bernard Skelton, better known by his nickname "Red." He is recognized as one of the funniest, most gifted comedians of all time. His comedy routine often included a series of pantomimes—a craft that he perfected to an art.

Skelton once did a skit entitled, "An Old Man Watches a Parade." In it he portrayed an elderly man who is evidently a veteran of a war of years ago. He stands watching the parade; though somewhat bent with age, he still proudly holds the weapon that he used to carry in the service of his country. He watches intently as the various groups in the parade—bands, soldiers, civic organizations, etc.—pass by. He waves to them, apparently hoping that someone will notice him and recognize him as someone who has given himself in his country's service. But no one notices; nobody seems to care. Everyone ignores him amidst all the noise, music, and activity.

Finally the old man can stand it no longer. He's tired of being just a spectator. So with a great deal of effort he leaves the crowd on the sidelines and joins those who are part of the procession. He wants to make sure everyone knows whose side he's on.

As we take these emblems of the Lord's Supper, we are to be more than just passive observers. We are not only to remember Jesus' sacrifice; we must resolve to be living sacrifices. We are not just to think about Jesus as he carried the cross; each of us must determine to carry his own cross. We are not to think only of Jesus' love for us; we are to resolve to love each other more deeply.

Exodus 32:26 records how Moses stood before the Israelites following the tragic incident involving the golden calf and uttered this challenge: "Whoever is for the Lord, come to me." The *King James Version* reads, "Who is on the Lord's side? let him come unto me." We are not to be spectators on the sidelines. We are to be part of the parade, boldly showing to the world whose side we are on. We are the Lord's people. We are on the Lord's side.

Make it Your Own

Do you know a story about a parade that you participated in, helped organize, or watched? Have you ever seen a particularly memorable parade (such as the Macy's Thanksgiving Day parade in New York City)? Use that story to begin this talk.

DATE USED _____

No Off Season

Our two sons have been avid sports card collectors for some time now. Ever since they became old enough to understand sports (particularly baseball, basketball, and football) and follow the careers of some of the outstanding players, they have developed and perfected ways to organize their collections and keep track of changes in the value of the various cards. (If only I'd had that kind of interest in my cards when I was their age!)

Much of their interest in specific cards hinges on the specific sport that is in season. During baseball season, for example, those cards get a lot more attention than the other cards do. When football season begins in the fall, the baseball cards are benched.

The observance of Communion is not a seasonal practice. It is not linked to any time of year or any special holiday. Paul writes, *"Whenever* you eat this bread and drink this cup, you proclaim the Lord's death until he comes" (1 Corinthians 11:26). The precedent of the New Testament church indicates that this was done each Lord's Day (Acts 20:7).

41

Does this frequency increase the likelihood that the Lord's Supper will mean less and less, and become a thoughtless, mechanical ritual? Hardly. This frequency means that regardless of how calm or how harried the days of the previous week may have been, the message of the Supper (the atoning death of Jesus for our sins) is meant to maintain a never-ending hold on our lives as Christians. He is Lord, regardless of the season of life we are currently experiencing—whether a time of gentle spring breezes or the onslaught of a bitter winter storm.

We are reminded that any circumstance we encounter in life will be encountered better by bringing the lordship of Jesus into the picture. Likewise, any circumstance that we try to navigate while ignoring that lordship will only become more confusing and frustrating.

The advice Paul gives to Timothy about preaching the Word is also good to apply to the observance of the Lord's Supper: "in season and out of season" (2 Timothy 4:2).

Make it Your Own

Can you think of an example of something you do (such as a certain hobby or a trip somewhere) that is seasonal? Use that illustration to begin this meditation.

DATE USED _____

42

No One Left Out

ROMANS 3:23; 2 CORINTHIANS 5:14, 15

When I was in elementary school, we almost always spent our recess playing softball. The usual procedure was to choose two captains who would then alternate in selecting boys to be on their teams. Most of the time there were two or three boys who were not really that good at softball. They were always the last to be picked, and one of them (being the only one left after the others were chosen) was dismissed to go and find something else to do to occupy his time.

Though I was not by any means a great player, neither was I considered as one of the rejects. It probably never occurred to me or to any of us, once the teams were chosen and the game began, how much it really hurt the one boy who was left out and not allowed to play with the others. Did he go off and play with the other kids, or did he find a place to hide and cry away his disappointment? What was it like for him when he went home and was asked by his mom or dad how the day went?

One of the most significant words in the Bible is also one of the shortest—the three-letter word *all*. While it appears in some of the bad news portions of Scripture (such as Romans 3:23—"All have sinned and fall short of the glory of God"), it also appears in good news verses such as 2 Corinthians 5:14 ("one died for *all*").

When Jesus died, he died for *all* the sins of *all* people of *all* history. Pontius Pilate, the chief priests, the Pharisees and Sadducees, the Roman soldiers—no matter how they treated him, he treated them with unconditional love by bearing the death penalty for their sins. Even though "he came to that which was his own, but his own did not receive him" (John 1:11), he died for them. No one was left out. No one was so evil, so corrupt, so steeped in sin, that Jesus was not willing to give his life for them.

Make it Your Own

Do you know a story that tells what it felt like for you or someone else to be left out of a particular event, activity, or group? Tell that story at the beginning of this meditation.

As we come to this time of Communion, let us remember that we are not on Jesus' team because we were good enough to deserve getting picked. Not one of us is good enough; all of us qualify as rejects. Yet Jesus was the one "despised and rejected by men" (Isaiah 53:3) that we could be accepted into the family of God. We're not left out anymore.

DATE USED _____

Our Sitting High Priest

Hebrews 10:11, 12

Our daughter took a job last summer in a Christian bookstore to earn some money for college. The job required her to be on her feet for most of the day, since she worked either at the cash register or in the book section of the store, straightening the shelves or helping customers find items they needed. Needless to say, when she got home, one of the first things she wanted to do was remove her shoes and get off of her feet! But even then, her job was not finished; she had to go back and do it all over again the next day. And when she left for college, the routine passed to someone else.

The seemingly never-ending aspect of her job—and of many others—can be likened to the never-ending work of the Old Testament priesthood. Hebrews 10:11, 12 contrasts their work with the finished work of Jesus: "Day after day every priest stands and performs his religious duties; again and again he offers the same sacrifices, which can never take away sins. But when this priest had offered for all time one sacrifice for sins, he sat down at the right hand of God."

Note how the contrast is set forth: the Old Covenant priest *stands* (present tense, since those sacrifices were still going on when the writer of Hebrews penned this); the New Covenant priest (Jesus) *sat down*. Why? Simple: his work was done; as Jesus himself stated from the cross, "It is finished." The *one sacrifice for sins* had been offered.

For this reason, Jesus is now off his feet. His atoning work as our high priest is done. We who recognize that this work was done to save us gather here weekly in his name and in his honor.

Are we tempted to think that the repetition of the observance of the Supper can become the kind of vain repetition about which Jesus warned us concerning prayer? Vain repetition describes the work of the Old Covenant high priest, who at times must have longed for some relief from the daily routine of sacrifice upon sacrifice. The repetition of the Lord's Supper is one that we can gladly, gratefully practice—as a memorial to the one sacrifice that took away all sins of all people.

Make it Your Own

Do you have a job (or have you ever had a job) that requires you to be on your feet for extended periods of time? Use such a story to begin this talk.

DATE USED _____

OUR SPIRITUAL STRING

2 PETER 1:5-9

Why is it that some things are easy to remember and others seem easy to forget? And why is it that the items easy to remember are often of little real significance, while the ones easy to forget are those that get us in the proverbial hot water?

People have developed various methods (known as "mnemonic devices") for remembering certain facts, dates, or responsibilities that they can't afford to forget. Probably the most familiar is tying a string around one's finger. For me, something almost always has to be written down if I'm going to remember to take care of it. In our home we have an erasable board hanging in the kitchen, on which to write memorable messages. The problem, of course, is that sometimes we forget to look at the board!

Peter describes one who is not maturing in Christlikeness as someone who is "nearsighted and blind, and has forgotten that he has been cleansed from his past sins" (2 Peter 1:9). We wonder how anyone could forget something so wondrous as being cleansed from one's past sins. Herein lies one of the reasons for the weekly observance of the Lord's Supper; it is the spiritual string around our finger that reminds us who we are and whose we are—that we are not our own, for we have been "bought at a price" (1 Corinthians 6:20).

We need this weekly reminder that we have not earned a place at this table. We have received it in spite of the fact that we are totally incapable of earning a spot. We are here solely because of *Jesus'* body and *Jesus'* blood.

Perhaps you've heard someone say, "Why observe Communion *every* Lord's Day? Doesn't that make it become too routine or commonplace? Doesn't it lose its meaning?" It's interesting that those who pose such questions may be part of a church that receives an offering every Lord's Day, yet no one seems worried that *that* practice may become too routine or lose its meaning. (For that matter, why go to church *every* Sunday?)

If we are going to be reminded to give every Sunday, then we ought to be reminded of how much we have been given—by the only One who had the power to give it.

Make it Your Own

Is there something specific that you do to help you remember important items? Was there something that you used to do (in school, for example) to help you remember important information? Use that story to introduce this meditation.

DATE USED _____

OUR SPIRITUAL SUNRISE

1 CORINTHIANS 11:26

For many of us, watching a sunrise means more than just the beginning of another day. The sight can be associated with particularly memorable occasions in our lives, such as a strikingly beautiful sunrise witnessed during a vacation trip, or an especially meaningful Easter Sunday service.

From the annals of American history comes the following account of an incident that took place at the signing of the United States Constitution in 1787. Much discussion and deliberation had taken place regarding the contents of this revolutionary document. Finally the state delegations voted to give unanimous approval to the Constitution. As the signing of the final draft was taking place, Benjamin Franklin made the last public remarks recorded. James Madison described them as follows:

Whilst the last members were signing it Doctor Franklin looking toward the President's Chair, at the back of which a . . . sun happened to be painted, observed to a few members near him, that Painters have found it difficult to distinguish in their art a rising from a setting sun. I have, said he, often and often in the course of the Session, and the vicissitudes of my hopes and fears as to its issue, looked at that

behind the President without being able to tell
whether it was rising or setting: But now at length I
have the happiness to know that it is a rising and not
a setting sun. (From Clarence B. Carson, *The Rebirth
of Liberty: The Founding of the American Republic,
1760-1800.* New Rochelle: Arlington House, 1973.)

We live in a time when some skeptics
claim that the sun is setting on the church.
They believe that the church is no longer
relevant. And as individual Christians, each
of us experiences dry spells—times that
shake our convictions and make us wonder
if the sun is rising or setting on our faith.

To have this time of Communion on the
first day of the week is like a spiritual sunrise for us. We begin the week reminding
ourselves who is in charge. The head of the
church has not abdicated his position, nor
can he be voted out of office. Paul tells us,
"Whenever you eat this bread and drink this
cup, you proclaim the Lord's death *until he
comes*" (1 Corinthians 11:26). Our best days
are not behind us; they're ahead of us!

The Lord's Supper reminds us that, for the
church and for the Christian, the sun is
never setting. The sun is always rising.

DATE USED _____

Make it Your Own

*Do you know a
story about a
particularly beau-
tiful or memorable
sunrise? Use that
story with this
meditation.*

OUR TRAINING TABLE

1 CORINTHIANS 9:24-27

I never participated much in sports during my elementary and high-school years. The only school team I played much on was my eighth-grade basketball team. Since most of our games were played in the evening, following the dinner hour, our coach gave us clear instructions about what we should and should not eat prior to the game. The key was to eat *light*; eating the wrong kind of food (something too greasy or heavy) was just asking for problems on the court.

At the college and professional levels, athletes are often assigned to a training table where their diet is strictly controlled, particularly if they need to lose weight in order to get in shape and make the team. The alternative is getting cut and spending the season on the sidelines.

Paul drew important spiritual lessons from the world of athletics. Were he a speaker in a congregation somewhere today, he might well use the local sports news to make a point. The Corinthians, to whom Paul wrote two of the letters found in the New Testament, were familiar with what were called the Isthmian games, held every other year and considered second in importance only to the Greek Olympic games. Paul informed them about the importance of self-discipline and training in the Christian life. At stake is the prize of "a crown that will last forever" (1 Corinthians 9:25).

The Lord's Supper may be considered as a kind of spiritual training table, intended to keep us fit for "the race marked out for us" (Hebrews 12:1). We need to be here each Lord's Day to stay in shape. Chances are good that if we are failing to meet our responsibility to be present at this table, we are weak in meeting other responsibilities of the Christian life as well.

The discipline that is required to give this table priority is the discipline that we need to live for Christ each day—facing every circumstance and every decision in light of the fact that we are in training for eternity.

Make it Your Own

Do you have a story about the importance of training for an athletic event or to make a team? Tell that story to introduce this meditation.

DATE USED _____

52

OUT OF PLACE

ISAIAH 64:6; 61:10

My wife and I were leaving the stands after a high-school football game when we happened to see one of our friends from church. He had come from work and was still wearing a three-piece suit and a tie— not the normal apparel for a football game! I commented on how nice he looked compared to everyone else in their more casual attire. He definitely stood out like the proverbial sore thumb.

Despite the fact that we may dress much the same as the people with whom we worship, we should never forget that it is only by the grace of God that we can be clothed with the proper spiritual attire that allows us to come before this table. As Isaiah the prophet reminds us, "All our righteous acts are like filthy rags . . . and like the wind our sins sweep us away" (Isaiah 64:6). If somehow our spiritual condition without God could be reflected by the clothes we wear, how disgusting we would look!

But God has graciously reclothed us. He has given us the opportunity to exchange our filthy rags for his "garments of salvation"—his "robe of righteousness" (Isaiah 61:10). This is just a part of the total makeover we receive when we realize how out of place our sins cause us to look in the presence of a pure and holy God, and when we acknowledge that Jesus is the only one who can take care of our sorry state.

Hear Jesus' counsel to the church in Laodicea. First, there is the problem: "You say, 'I am rich; I have acquired wealth and do not need a thing.' But you do not realize that you are wretched, pitiful, poor, blind and naked" Revelation 3:17). Then comes the solution: "I counsel you to buy from me gold refined in the fire, so you can become rich; and white clothes to wear, so you can cover your shameful nakedness; and salve to put on your eyes, so you can see" (v. 18).

The Lord's Supper reminds us of the grace that has provided us with the clothes we wear—a designer label fashioned by the grand designer himself. These godly garments are meant to be worn well so that others will want to wear them too.

Make it Your Own

Have you ever been in a situation where you felt out of place because of how you looked or because of something you said or did? Use that story to begin this talk.

DATE USED _____

54

PAY ATTENTION!

LUKE 22:19-24, HEBREWS 12:2

One of the challenges facing a Christian service camp staff is to devise ways of getting the campers' attention. With a group numbering around sixty or seventy, this isn't always easy. One technique that seemed to work fairly well was the hands-up rule. Whenever someone wanted the campers to settle down, he or she would raise a hand and say, "When the hands go up, the mouths go closed." As silence began to prevail, other campers took notice and raised their hands; and soon some semblance of order was restored.

Consider the degree of attention that Jesus' disciples paid to what was going on around them on the night when Jesus instituted the Lord's Supper. The tension in the room grew as the Passover meal progressed, and as it became apparent to the twelve that this was not going to be a typical Passover. Emotions likely reached the breaking point when Jesus announced, "The hand of him who is going to betray me is with mine on the table" (Luke 22:21). Luke notes, as do Matthew and Mark, that the disciples began to ask which of them would commit such an act of treason. At this point, only Luke provides us with an additional insight into the concerns of Jesus' followers: "Also a dispute arose among them as to which of them was considered to be greatest" (Luke 22:24).

Just think: Jesus was on the verge of an agonizing death by crucifixion through which he would rescue lost mankind forever from eternal condemnation—and his disciples were quibbling over who among them would be the greatest! Like mischievous children at camp, their attention had been diverted from the One in charge.

As we come to this time of Communion now, what items over the past week have diverted our attention from the One in charge? What circumstances have seemed larger than he or beyond his control? In what situations have we listened to the world's counsel rather Christ's? Where have we been childish rather than childlike?

As we look at the bread and the cup this morning, let us also "fix our eyes on Jesus, the author and perfecter of our faith" (Hebrews 12:2). Let us give full attention to the One who allowed nothing to distract him from carrying out his Father's plan.

DATE USED _____

Make it Your Own

Do you know a story that describes a situation where someone failed to pay attention to what was going on around him or her? Use that story to open this meditation.

PERFECTION

2 CORINTHIANS 5:21

During my first year as a student in graduate school, I worked part-time in a local pharmacy. One day, while putting away an order of medicines that had arrived, I came across a packing slip on which was written the following message:

> My goal is to pick your order accurately and to pack every item carefully so that it reaches you in perfect condition. I take pride in my work and appreciate your help in making me a better team player. Have I hit the mark? Please let me know.

No one comes to this Communion table in perfect condition. We must confess that we have the missed mark many times, in spite of our most worthwhile goals and desires. We do not come because our efforts are exemplary. Often, our arrows don't even come close to the bull's-eye.

Why do we come? We come because of someone else, one whose life *was* in perfect condition—in every thought, word, and deed. Someone who really could take pride in his work. Someone who never missed the mark. Someone whose arrows always struck the bull's-eye dead center.

Who is he? He is the same someone who was crucified and treated as though he were the worst kind of lawbreaker. Throughout his life he never missed the target. Then he laid down his life for all who have—in other words, the whole world.

"God made him who had no sin to be sin for us, so that in him we might become the righteousness of God" (2 Corinthians 5:21).

At this table, we do not take pride in our work, but we offer deepest thanks for the work of Jesus. And we recognize that it is only through his work in us that we can all become better team players in his kingdom.

Make it Your Own

Recall a job performance evaluation, formal or informal, that made you question the quality of your work. Substitute that story for this one.

DATE USED _____

REAL POWER

1 CORINTHIANS 1:23, 24

Baseball fans were in ecstasy during 1998 at the exploits of Mark McGwire of the St. Louis Cardinals. McGwire shattered the single-season home run record by hitting an astonishing 70 home runs.

When the Cardinals came to Cincinnati in July, our family decided to get in on the McGwire mania. We drove down to Cinergy Field early enough to watch batting practice. McGwire didn't disappoint us, hitting several pitches into the upper deck and producing a series of *oohs* and *aahs* from the fans. People are impressed by that kind of power.

Consider what Paul has to tell us about power: "We preach Christ crucified: . . . to those whom God has called, both Jews and Greeks, Christ the power of God and the wisdom of God" (1 Corinthians 1:23, 24). How can someone crucified—someone hanging helplessly on a cross—express the power of God? Paul could have named many other events from Jesus' life as evidence for God's power: he walked on water, he healed the sick, he fed the multitudes. Yet at the cross, where Jesus seemed to be weakest and most vulnerable—there, says

Paul, we see Christ as the power of God. No wonder the cross is a stumbling block to some and foolishness to others. This is not how we tend to think of power, is it?

Christ's power at the cross was not power shown through aggression or fanfare; it was power demonstrated through *surrender*— refusing to do what he could have done—so that others would be saved. Jesus *could* have called upon his Father to save him from the cross—*could* have summoned twelve legions of angels—but he didn't. At the cross Jesus yielded his power—the power that had delivered others—in order to carry out his Father's purpose. He demonstrated power, not by asserting his rights, but by giving them away.

Business people sometimes speak of having a power lunch at which important decisions or issues are considered. This Lord's Supper is a power supper for us. It reminds us of how real power is gained—not by demanding our rights, but by yielding them to Jesus and serving him as Lord. This is a battle where victory comes through *surrender*.

Make it Your Own

Can you think of someone in sports, business, or other professions who has demonstrated what the world tends to think of as power? Use that story at the beginning of this talk.

DATE USED _____

RENEWED VOWS

A couple who once lived next door to our family came up with a unique way to commemorate their fiftieth wedding anniversary. They had an eight-millimeter film of a portion of their wedding in 1946 converted to a video cassette. Then they made a videotape of the ceremony fifty years later during which they renewed their vows to one another, and placed that immediately after the 1946 material. My wife and I watched the video with the couple during a visit not long after it was made. We could see how happy they were with the way it turned out, and justifiably so.

The Lord's Supper provides us the opportunity every Lord's Day to renew our vows to the One whose bride is the church—the One to whom every Christian is spiritually united in a bond that is close enough and holy enough to be likened in Scripture to marriage. At this table, we span not just fifty years, but two thousand years, as we remember the pain, the agony, the suffering, and, most of all, the love expressed at Calvary.

Is there any question that we need such a time of renewal—and need it weekly? We live in a world where marriage is under attack—both in the natural and spiritual realms. It is a world that is increasingly hostile and resistant to our Husband and a world that dangles before us numerous seductions to lure us away from him. Temptations to spiritual adultery abound.

In Revelation 2:4 Jesus tells the Ephesian Christians that they have lost their first love. This table gives us the opportunity to renew and reaffirm that first love as we remember how much Jesus loves his bride.

As you take these emblems today, picture yourself before Jesus, renewing your vows to him in words something like these: "I take you, Jesus, as my Lord and my Savior. I pledge myself to be true to you in sickness and in health, in joy and in sorrow, in prosperity and in adversity, and, forsaking all others, to serve you alone as my master— not till death do us part, but till death shall bring us together."

Make it Your Own

Do you know a story about a renewal of vows made between a husband and wife? Use that story to begin this talk.

DATE USED _____

REST STOP

MATTHEW 11:28-30

"Can we rest now?" That's what our children used to ask me when we were running around outdoors or wrestling on the floor with each other. (Now that they're older, it tends to be *me* who's asking with greater frequency, "Can we rest now?")

Anyone who has ever driven a long distance knows the importance of taking a rest stop—if not at one of the roadside areas so named, then at a restaurant, park, or similar location where everyone, especially the driver, can relax. It is necessary to do that so that all can arrive safely (and sanely!) at their destination.

Rest in the spiritual realm is no less important. The pace of modern life can be such that we often find ourselves on a high-speed expressway of activities, meetings, and deadlines, looking for an exit anywhere. Yet none seems to come. We can experience a form of spiritual road rage, getting impatient and frustrated with the people whom we think are interfering with our progress.

The Lord's Supper provides us with a much-needed spiritual rest stop each first day of the week. Here we exit from the cares and pressures of the world to come before the table spread by the one who tells us, "Come to me, all you who are weary and burdened, and I will give you rest" (Matthew 11:28). While Jesus did not speak these words when he instituted the Lord's Supper, they are words that call our attention to one of the blessings we receive from this Supper. This is a time of refreshment and rejuvenation, where we give our weary souls the rest and nourishment they need before we enter once again the fast lane of daily life. After all, we want to arrive safely at our destination too.

This thought of rest is expressed well in the words of a hymn that is often sung at Communion time:

Beneath the cross of Jesus I fain would take my stand,
The shadow of a mighty Rock within a weary land;
A home within the wilderness, A rest upon the way,
From the burning of the noonday heat, And the burden of the day.

As we take these emblems today, may we also take the rest that Jesus offers.

Make it Your Own

Try to think of a story that illustrates the importance of rest (perhaps a humorous story about needing a rest stop during travels with your family). Use that story with this meditation.

DATE USED _____

64

SELF-HELPLESS

LUKE 22:19, 20

I was traveling with a group of men to a three-day outdoor retreat. One of the men in our group had been to the retreat before and assured us that he knew the way. (You probably already know where this story is headed!) Yes, despite his professed confidence in his memory of the route to the campsite, the rest of us found our skepticism growing as we journeyed over roads that we will likely never see again. We tried to persuade our friend to stop and ask for directions, but he "just knew we were about there" or "felt we were getting closer." Eventually (without help) we did arrive at the campsite, though we were hardly impressed with our friend's version of "Destination Unknown."

Why is it so hard sometimes to admit we need help? Such stubbornness is often associated with men, but it is actually manifested at an early stage in everyone. Most of us have watched a child insist on doing a particular activity "all by myself," adamantly refusing assistance from anyone. Let's be honest: every generation has been, to some extent, a "me" generation. This obsession is currently demonstrated by the self-help phenomenon.

The message of this Communion table is not one that encourages self-help. On the contrary, this table confronts us with how helpless we are. Think of the words Jesus spoke as he instituted the Lord's Supper: "This is my body given for you" and "This cup is the new covenant in my blood, which is poured out for you" (Luke 22:19, 20). Note the pronouns: *"my* body . . . for *you"* and *"my* blood . . . for *you."* At the cross Jesus did for us what we never could have done for ourselves. "While we were still sinners," Paul reminds us in Romans 5:8, "Christ died for us"—because he could not wait until we *weren't* sinners to die for us.

The road to Heaven is not one that we can negotiate all by ourselves, depending on our skills and experience to get us there. We are helpless without Jesus. To think otherwise and thereby reject the assistance that has been offered is surely to travel at our own (eternal) risk.

Make it Your Own

Can you think of a time when someone (maybe you!) refused to ask for or get help with a certain task? Use that story to begin this meditation.

DATE USED _____

SOMETIMES IT HURTS

ISAIAH 6:1-5; LUKE 5:8

Like most children, I approached a visit to the dentist with a great deal of fear and trembling. In my case, part of the problem was the dentist himself. He was a rather cranky, ill-tempered older man, who did not have a high degree of patience with children (like me) who got fidgety and tended to squirm in his chair.

As I grew older, many of my anxieties about visiting the dentist began to lessen. For one thing, the aforementioned dentist died and we found a kinder, gentler man to go to. I also began to develop good brushing habits, which meant fewer (and many times no) cavities. Eventually I reached the point where I felt somewhat comfortable in the dentist's chair.

We come to this Communion table once a week—far more frequently than any of us visit the dentist. However, the purpose of this frequency is not to make us feel comfortable before this table. It is not designed to help us reach the point where we become "good" at taking Communion, or where we simply "relax and don't feel a thing," as the dentist usually tells us to do.

The fact is, there may be times when coming to this table will move us to tears—when the struggles of the previous week have left us feeling sifted by Satan (Luke 22:31) or when we reflect on our unworthiness to be treated as God has so graciously treated us. Like Isaiah, who "saw the Lord seated on a throne, high and exalted" and saw himself as "ruined" (Isaiah 6:1-5) or Peter, who was overwhelmed by his sinfulness in the presence of Jesus' miracle-working power (Luke 5:8, 9), we may question whether we should be where we are.

However, there should be no question that we have come to the right place and to the right person—the great physician. If we come in a spirit of joy and celebration, he will meet us; if we come afraid or overwhelmed by fears or failures, he will meet us. Whether we are uplifted or upset, this is where we need to be. Whether we have practiced good spiritual hygiene over the past week or whether we have cavities that need to be filled, we ought to keep our appointment at the Lord's table.

Yes, sometimes it hurts to be at this table. But it hurts much more to ignore it.

DATE USED _____

Make it Your Own

Do you have a story to tell about an uncomfortable experience that you, a family member, or a friend had with a dentist? Use that story at the beginning of this talk.

SOUL WORK

HEBREWS 2:18; 4:15; 1 JOHN 4:4

A car accident just isn't the way one wants to begin a weekend. I had just picked up my son from a high-school activity. Turning out of the parking lot, we joined the slowly moving traffic. We had gone only a short distance when we heard a banging noise some distance behind us. It was followed by a series of increasingly louder bangs; and before we realized what was going on, the bang was coming from our vehicle! Our van was the last vehicle hit in a four-car collision that left our tailgate and rear bumper damaged, but everything else, including my son and me, in good shape.

There followed the unfortunate but necessary steps that one has to take to get a damaged vehicle fixed. We called our insurance company, took the van to the claims center to get an estimate, and then made an appointment to get the body work done. All the steps went fairly smoothly and within a month or so after the accident happened, no trace of the accident could be seen on the van.

What happens to us when we get rear-ended or side-swiped spiritually? There's no question that some of us gathered here for worship have taken some real hits from Satan over the past week. Things happened that we weren't expecting. Interruptions kept us from accomplishing all we had planned to do. We may look fine on the outside, but inside we've been crunched, or at least dented. We may be dressed in our Sunday best, but we feel the impact of our Monday-through-Saturday worst. Some of the damage can be attributed to our own carelessness or stubbornness, but some of it was not our fault at all. Regardless of the cause, we're hurting. We need soul work.

And who better to go to for this work than one who was "tempted in every way, just as we are" (Hebrews 4:15) and who is therefore "able to help those who are being tempted" (Hebrews 2:18)? The emblems at this table remind us that Jesus took Satan's best shot—his hardest hit *(death)*—and could not be beaten!

As Jesus' followers today, we are not exempt from Satan's hits, but neither are we exempt from the Savior's help. There is no question who has the upper hand: "The one who is in you is greater than the one who is in the world" (1 John 4:4).

Make it Your Own

Have you ever been in an accident that required some amount of body work? (If not, my sincere congratulations!) Tell about your experience to begin this meditation.

DATE USED _____

70

TABLE OF FORGETFULNESS

HEBREWS 8:12

When our daughter graduated from high school not long ago, we hosted an open house for her. To prepare for the guests who would be coming, she set up what was curiously referred to (in the lingo of her friends) as a "shrine"—a table on which was placed pictures, awards, and other objects highlighting her achievements. Occasionally some of these graduation "shrines" also feature photographs of the student when he or she was much younger, thus providing a kind of pictorial history of the student—something of particular interest to his or her friends.

One often sees a similar table of memorabilia at an anniversary or birthday celebration, particularly when it marks a significant milestone such as fifty years of marriage or a ninetieth birthday. At such occasions, the greater the time span being celebrated, the more interest the pictures seem to spark. It is quite fascinating to see how people looked and dressed and lived years ago.

We often think of the Communion table as a table of remembrance. Jesus would have us do so, for he spoke the familiar words, "Do this in remembrance of me," when he instituted the Supper (1 Corinthians 11:24, 25). Many Communion tables are inscribed with these words.

However, this is also a table of forgetfulness. Unlike the memorabilia tables described earlier, which call us to remember someone's past, the Communion table calls us to acknowledge that God has *forgotten* our past. Through the blood of his Son he has provided a fully atoning sacrifice. The New Covenant that was established by that blood has as one of its hallmarks this promise: "I will forgive their wickedness and will remember their sins no more" (Hebrews 8:12). Scripture includes some rather striking images of just how sweeping this forgiveness is ("as far as the east is from the west" in Psalm 103:12; hurling all our iniquities "into the depths of the sea" in Micah 7:19).

How wondrous is the love of God! He knows everything about us, yet is willing to forgive and forget what we have done. Let us take these emblems in remembrance of him who remembers our sins no more.

Make it Your Own

Have you ever seen a table such as the one described at the beginning of this meditation? Do you have a story about something special that you noticed on such a table? Tell that story to begin this meditation.

DATE USED _____

72

TABLE OF SURPRISES

LUKE 15:17-24

My fortieth birthday was a memorable one, primarily because of the surprise that was part of the occasion. A girl from the church where I had previously served arranged to meet my wife and me at a restaurant that was about two hours away from each of us.

When we arrived at the restaurant, we were greeted not only by the girl and her parents but by a number of other people from the church, who had planned this very special surprise. I received several gifts, most of which called attention in one way or another to the milestone I had reached. We all enjoyed a memorable evening—one that made hitting forty much less painful.

At first it may seem odd to think of the Communion table as a table of surprises; after all, we gather here at the same time every week, and we partake of the same food. Where's the surprise? The surprise is found in what this table reminds us about why we are here.

Consider Jesus' parable of the prodigal son, particularly the contrast between how this young man *expected* to be treated and how he *was* treated. First, he left home expecting to find the high life and instead ended up living the sty life—with the pigs. Second, he came back home expecting to be made one of the hired servants, and found himself receiving a hero's welcome from his father! Talk about surprises!

Think of the irony. When the son thought that he didn't deserve his father's love anymore, that was when his father expressed his love most exuberantly. When he thought he was least worthy to come home, that was when he was the most welcome. When he figured his father wouldn't be able to stand the sight of his face, that was when Dad was the happiest to see him.

That is exactly how God has treated us. In spite of sins and failures too numerous for us to count, he has forgiven us and invited us to this covenant meal. We should be as amazed that God would give his Son to die for us as the prodigal son was to see his father kill the fatted calf for him. May we never lose the sense of wonder—of surprise!—at all that this table represents.

Make it Your Own

Do you know a story about something that was done to surprise you, someone in your family, a friend, or a fellow employee at work? Use that story to begin this meditation.

DATE USED _____

THE CLEAN PLATE CLUB

MATTHEW 23:25, 26

Like numerous other parents, my wife and I found it a real challenge sometimes to get our children to eat their meals. My wife used a ploy (one which I think she learned from her mother) of encouraging our children to be part of what she called the "clean plate club," by eating everything set before them. There was never, to my knowledge, any package of benefits associated with membership in this club (no membership card was issued, no prizes were given), but that didn't matter. Just knowing that they belonged to the club seemed to satisfy our children.

Whenever we gather before the Communion table, we are not expected to clean our plates; the Lord's Supper is not that kind of meal. We are expected, however, to take a good close look at the kind of spiritual diet that we have been maintaining. What kind of food have we allowed to enter our minds over the past week? We must not think that we can fill our minds with the world's junk food from Monday through Saturday, then come properly prepared for the Lord's table. Think about it: do we give as much attention to our inward preparation for worship as we do to our outward preparation?

The Lord's Supper can be, in some instances, a time to confess our sins, remembering the only One through whom forgiveness of sins is possible. But something is wrong if that kind of inward cleansing is occurring *only* when we come to take the Lord's Supper. Just as children have to learn to clean their plates every day, we have to learn to "clean the inside of the cup and dish" (Matthew 23:26) on a daily basis.

We would also do well to develop the discipline of keeping the inside from getting dirty in the first place by avoiding those circumstances that are most apt to soil us spiritually. Then we can come to this table with an attitude of thanksgiving for the victory over sin's power and influence that God's Spirit provides. (Membership in this clean plate club is demonstrated by how we behave when we've *left* the table!)

This is not a table for the sinless, but for those who have made a commitment to sin less.

Make it Your Own

Do you have a particular technique that you use to persuade your children to eat their meals? Talk about that at the beginning of this meditation.

DATE USED _____

76

THE MATTER OF THE HEART

The March 14, 1996, edition of the *Wall Street Journal* carried the touching story of a girl, age 16, who received a heart transplant. The story described the long, tedious process involved in obtaining a transplant and the emotional roller coaster that the family rode until finally, one day, the wonderful news came that a heart for this girl had indeed become available. The story tells of how, when the girl was fully on the road to recovery, she asked the doctors and nurses about the donor and the donor's family. They informed her that the donor's name and family had to be held strictly confidential. They suggested that the girl write a letter, which they promised to forward to the donor's family. This is what the letter said:

Dear Family,

I am the recipient of the heart that you were generous enough to donate in the midst of your own personal family tragedy. I can only imagine how difficult it must have been for you to suffer the loss, and then to offer the organs so that other people could live.

I feel a great responsibility to live my life so that your sacrifice will be worthwhile, and I can't express to you the gratitude that I and my family feel for saving my life. If you ever desire to contact me, I would be more than happy to know you. And I hope that you know that I feel responsible to bring honor to your family as well as mine.

Several comparisons could be made between what this girl wrote and what Christians have experienced. Every Christian has received a new heart—a second chance—thanks to the Great Physician. When we come to this table, our thoughts can be expressed as follows:

Dear Lord,

I am the recipient of the heart that you were generous enough to provide at the cost of your only Son. I can only imagine how difficult it must have been for you to suffer the loss, and to offer him at the cross that other people could live.

I feel a great responsibility to live my life so that your sacrifice will be worthwhile, and I can't express to you the gratitude that I feel for saving my soul. Wherever you lead me—whatever you would do with my life—I would be more than happy to do it. I pledge myself to bring honor to your Son and to your family—the church.

Make it Your Own

Do you have a story about an organ transplant and how grateful the recipient was to get the organ he or she received? Tell that story instead of this one.

DATE USED _____

78

THE ONE IN FRONT OF YOU

ROMANS 12:15

When we attended one of our son's high-school football games this past fall, we sat behind a family we didn't know. As the game progressed, our team tried to move the ball by using a few more passes. One of the receivers was getting open, but he was having a hard time catching the ball. Two or three passes bounced off his chest or shoulder pads and fell incomplete. With each miss, the crowd's groans got louder and their patience thinner (mine included). At one point my wife, who had started a conversation with the woman in front of us, nudged me and said, "That's the receiver's mother." I winced—and tried to groan thereafter with a little less intensity. Eventually the boy did make several nice catches.

It's easy at times to ignore the feelings or perspectives of the people around us, especially when we think they should be doing their job better, or when their failure to do so poses an inconvenience to us. We get impatient with the individuals involved, whether it be a slow driver, a highway construction crew, or a new and unsure clerk at the store. Too often our vision is entirely self-centered. We are too engrossed in our own concerns to put ourselves in the other person's shoes or to be Christlike in a moment when someone could use a dose of Christlikeness!

Whenever we take the Lord's Supper, we take it individually. Each person must examine himself or herself, as the Scripture says. And yet this is a family meal. In the passage from 1 Corinthians 11 where Paul gives instructions concerning the Lord's Supper, four times he mentions being "together."

That togetherness is important to keep in mind, not only when we take the Lord's Supper, but between Sundays as well. The people with whom we eat—the single mother in front of us, the widower behind us, the bereaved family to our left—these are fellow pilgrims and strugglers on the road to Heaven. Our fellowship with them must extend beyond the moments spent together before this table. We are called to spend more than Sundays together; we are called to share *life* together—as instructed by Paul, we are to "Rejoice with those who rejoice; mourn with those who mourn" (Romans 12:15). Moments of fellowship away from the table will make the moments at the table even more meaningful.

Make it Your Own

Can you think of a time when you were impatient or careless with someone—perhaps in a situation where you discovered (to your chagrin) that you didn't have complete understanding of what was going on? Use that story to begin this talk.

DATE USED _____

80

THE VOICE

REVELATION 3:20

Many of us remember Frank Sinatra—one of the most well-known entertainers of modern times. The day after his death on May 15, 1998, the local newspaper announced his passing with the headline, "The Voice Goes Silent." Sinatra was nicknamed "The Voice" because of his enormous popularity and his redefinition of popular music, so the newspaper headline seemed an appropriate one.

That was the headline that the enemies of Jesus wanted to believe when they crucified him. "At last," they figured, "his voice has been silenced. John the Baptist called himself a voice crying in the wilderness, but someone shut him up. And now we've done the same to Jesus." Or so they thought.

Of course, that silence was shattered three days later when Jesus arose from the dead. His voice may have been quieted for a brief time, but it certainly had not been silenced. Today that voice remains strong and clear, as the words of Revelation 3:20 indicate: "Here I am! I stand at the door and knock. If anyone hears my voice and opens the door, I will come in and eat with him, and he with me."

Sometimes this verse is used to appeal to the unsaved to accept Christ. But Jesus is not addressing the unsaved; He's speaking to a church (at Laodicea). He's talking to Christians and saying to them and to us, "If any of *you* hear my voice . . ."

We live in a world where the voice of Jesus is sometimes very difficult to hear. Think of all the noise around us every day— the voices we hear clamoring for our attention. We need a quiet place—a closet, as it were—to be alone with Jesus and to listen to his voice.

Make it Your Own

Do you know a story about a famous singer such as Frank Sinatra, or about any person (a singer or actor) whose voice was especially famous or recognizable? Use that story to begin this devotion.

This Lord's Supper provides us with just such a place—a place we can enter every Lord's Day, a place where we can hear Jesus' voice and eat and drink in fellowship with him and he with us. We need to remember that if we cannot hear that voice, it isn't the voice's fault. It's because we've become too busy and too preoccupied to listen. For this is the voice that will never go silent.

DATE USED _____

THE WEIGHT LIFTER

1 PETER 2:24

A few years ago I injured my back while helping some friends move. I can recall the moment when it happened. I was trying to lift my end of a couch over the threshold of the building where we were going to store it. That extra strain did me in and laid me up! Since then I've had to be cautious about doing any especially heavy lifting. In some cases, just a slight (but awkward) twisting of my back has produced severe pain. So I've had to "just say no" to those occasional requests for assistance with lifting something that could be hazardous to my health. For the same reason, I've sometimes had to ask for help with an object rather than risk going it alone.

The load of one's sin is a load that is far too heavy for anyone to try to carry by himself. To attempt to do so is to invite irreparable spiritual damage. Only one person—Jesus Christ—could carry that burden. No one could help him, because the required sacrifice had to be a sinless one. Only Jesus met such a lofty criterion.

It is instructive to consider the two burdens that Jesus had to carry on the day he was crucified. The first was the burden of his cross. Apparently at one point during his struggle to the site of the crucifixion, Jesus stumbled and fell. A bystander, Simon of Cyrene, was commandeered to carry the cross the rest of the way (Mark 15:21).

When the crowd finally arrived at Golgotha, Jesus was nailed to his cross. There he carried the second burden—one that not Simon of Cyrene, nor any human being, could help him bear. It was the load of the world's sins, as he "bore our sins in his body on the tree" (1 Peter 2:24).

Just how heavy was that weight that Jesus was lifting and taking on himself when he died for the sins of the entire human race? We cannot begin to calculate it. All we need to know is that it was outweighed by the love that moved him to carry it.

As we take these emblems today, let us hear anew the call of Jesus to "take up the cross." Whatever that cross may entail, it cannot begin to compare with the demands associated with Jesus' cross. Our cross is ours alone; Jesus' cross was the cross of millions.

Make it Your Own

Do you have a story to tell about trying to lift a heavy object? Tell that one here.

DATE USED _____

84

Too Often?

2 Peter 1:12

Not long ago our older son received his driver's license. In the process of riding with our son during the time that he had his learner's permit, my wife and I tried to impress upon him how important certain elements of good, safe driving are (like fastening your seat belt before you do anything else, not following another vehicle too closely, etc.). Since a number of small children live in our neighborhood, we've also emphasized how necessary it is to drive slowly and alertly in our area.

I am sure that with many of these rules and regulations we have committed some degree of overkill, at least from our son's perspective. But there are certain essentials (and this is true of any area of life) that bear repeating simply because they are just that—*essentials*.

Some believe that taking the Lord's Supper on a weekly basis means taking it weakly because it begins to take on the nature of a meaningless routine. But this is giving the idea of frequency a negative connotation that it does not deserve. Would anyone dare to suggest that *daily* Bible study and *daily* prayer be discontinued because they may lose their meaning by such frequent occurrence? Or consider David's statement of commitment to prayer: "Evening, morning and noon I cry out in distress, and he hears my voice" (Psalm 55:17)—a pattern followed with fearless allegiance by Daniel (Daniel 6:10). Oh, for that kind of frequency among Christians today!

Peter wrote of the need to "always remind" his readers of the truths he conveyed in his second epistle—even though he noted that they were "firmly established" in these matters (2 Peter 1:12). For Peter, these essentials could never become so familiar that he would be wasting his time (and his ink) calling them to the attention of his readers. Essentials always bear repeating.

Is the weekly observance of Communion too often? It is never too often to remind ourselves of the most wonderful gift (Jesus) given to save the most unworthy recipients (us) from the most horrible punishment (Hell).

Make it Your Own

Do you know of a certain body of information that you have to communicate on a regular basis (or that has to be communicated to you) because it is so essential? Tell about that at the beginning of this talk.

DATE USED _____

TRIUMPH OF THE UNDERDOG

PHILIPPIANS 2:5-8

In 1982, Plymouth High School in Plymouth, Indiana, won the Indiana state high-school basketball tournament. Since Plymouth was a smaller town (population around 8,000 or so), this victory was quite an achievement.

The path to the state championship was marked by victories over schools from South Bend, Indianapolis, and Gary. Each time a team from one of the bigger cities was played, comments were made about David versus Goliath. And, in keeping with the biblical account, each time David won. With basketball as popular as it was (and still is) in Indiana, Plymouth's championship gave the 1982 team almost legendary status.

The stakes at the battle of Calvary were the highest they could be: the eternal destiny of humanity. Throughout his ministry, Jesus had consistently demonstrated power superior to Satan's. Every encounter with demonic forces went in favor of Jesus; in fact, he had amassed an unbeaten record.

Yet, at the cross, Jesus deliberately placed himself at a disadvantage. He subjected himself to defeat. He made it clear that he could have called on his Father for help, and more than twelve legions of angels would have immediately annihilated his foes (Matthew 26:53).

Why did someone who had been heretofore unbeatable become beatable? That is the very reason why Jesus came to earth: to save others at the expense of himself. He was treated as a loser so that we can win. He was treated as the lowest of criminals so that we may reign as kings. He became the underdog so that we can become champions. Paul explained this sacrifice with these words: "Your attitude should be the same as that of Christ Jesus: Who, being in very nature God, did not consider equality with God something to be grasped, but made himself nothing, taking the very nature of a servant, . . . he humbled himself and became obedient to death—even death on a cross!" (Philippians 2:5-8).

As we take these emblems today, let us remember how the Son of David placed himself in a position where, like his renowned ancestor, he had to commit his circumstances to God, believing that "the battle is the Lord's" (1 Samuel 17:47).

Make it Your Own

Can you think of an example of how an underdog team or individual won an unexpected victory? Use that story at the beginning of this talk.

DATE USED _____

88

WAKE-UP CALL

1 CORINTHIANS 11:29, 30

An incident occurred in our neighborhood not long ago—one that seems funny now, but was far from funny at the time it took place. A lady drove by our house, described a little girl, and asked if we had seen her. The girl had been missing for about four hours. We did not have to know the girl's family for the news to have a disturbing, numbing effect. Before long the air was filled with the sound of helicopters as police began to comb the area. Was the usual calm of our neighborhood about to be irreparably shattered?

As dusk began to fall, we heard the news that we had all hoped to hear—the girl had been found! She had been discovered *sleeping in her own house!* Apparently she had crawled behind a computer desk (perhaps during a game of hide and seek) and had not been found either by family members or the police.

In his instructions to the Corinthians concerning the Lord's Supper, Paul calls attention to the danger of eating and drinking "without recognizing the body of the Lord" (1 Corinthians 11:29). "That is why," he tells them, "many among you are weak and sick, and a number of you have fallen asleep" (v. 30). Some believe that Paul is speaking of the "sleep" of death. But it is also possible to understand his words as descriptive of a spiritual slumber that has the potential to desensitize the Corinthians to matters of eternal importance.

The increasingly secular world in which we spend our time between Lord's Days can deaden our spiritual senses. Like the little girl, we fall asleep and become oblivious to all that's going on around us: the people who need the Lord, the neighbors who are hurting, the friendships we often take for granted, the situations in which we need to step forward as Christ's ambassador.

Though most of us probably close our eyes before and after we partake of the Lord's Supper, we ought to use these moments as a time of reawakening and revitalization of the spirit. We need to keep our spiritual eyes always opened to the good things God has done for us (and continues to do) and to our responsibilities to be his faithful servants "until he comes."

Make it Your Own

Can you recall a humorous, embarrassing, or unusual incident that involved falling asleep? Use that story to begin this meditation.

DATE USED _____

90

What Do You See?

2 Corinthians 4:18

While I was in the seventh grade, I learned that I needed glasses. I can still remember when I put them on the first time. I didn't really notice anything particularly different until the optometrist told me to look across the street. Then I couldn't believe how much clearer everything looked! Obviously I had been missing a lot and didn't realize it.

When an unbeliever looks at the emblems of the Lord's Supper, what do you suppose he sees? Probably nothing more than a few pieces of bread (or a loaf, in some cases) and several small cups of grape juice (or again, in certain instances, a single cup). "What kind of supper is this?" he may wonder.

But once we put on spiritual glasses, our view of this Supper changes dramatically. Just as we no longer see Jesus "from a worldly point of view" (2 Corinthians 5:16), so we no longer view the objects associated with Jesus in the same way. Consider the story of the prophet Elisha, whose servant was terrified at the presence of the Aramean army around the city of Samaria. Elisha assured him, "Those who are with us are more than those who are with them." Then Elisha prayed, "O Lord, open his eyes so he may see." The Lord proceeded to open the servant's eyes so that he could see "the hills full of horses and chariots of fire all around Elisha" (2 Kings 6:15-17).

Here at the Lord's Supper, we take the bread and the juice; but with the aid of spiritual glasses we see much more. We see Calvary; we see the Son of God bleeding and dying in agony, bearing the punishment that should have been ours. We see the crowds jeering and mocking the One who was and is mankind's only hope of salvation. But we also see him risen from the grave, commissioning his disciples to carry on the task he began, and assuring them that his presence will sustain them "to the very end of the age" (Matthew 28:20).

At this table "we live by faith, not by sight" (2 Corinthians 5:7), yet by believing we are given a sight "not of this world." That sight, as Paul wrote to the Corinthian Christians, enables us to "fix our eyes not on what is seen, but on what is unseen. For what is seen is temporary, but what is unseen is eternal" (2 Corinthians 4:18).

Make it Your Own

Can you think of a story that illustrates the need for glasses (or contact lenses)? Use that illustration to open this meditation.

DATE USED _____

YOUR PLACE AT THE TABLE

1 CORINTHIANS 11:20-22

A couple of years ago we attended a high-school function that involved one of our children. Since a catered meal was to be served prior to the evening program, people were encouraged to send in reservations in order to get an accurate count. Yet, in spite of everyone's best efforts, some of the items on the menu were gone before everyone was served. A few of the unfortunate people at the end of the line who were left out were a bit disgruntled and asked for their money to be refunded. It was the only negative part of what was an otherwise enjoyable evening.

The Corinthian church held what was known as a "love feast" (today we would call it a "fellowship dinner") in conjunction with the observance of the Lord's Supper. This did not involve any catered meals; however, some individuals still felt left out, since many of the more well-to-do brought food for themselves but failed to share their bounty with the poorer members of the church. Such a selfish, thoughtless attitude was sapping the sense of unity from the observance of the Lord's Supper.

As we take the Supper together now,

observe that everyone receives approximately the same amount of bread and juice. Those who have been Christians for many years do not receive a larger portion, or have themselves distinguished from everyone else in some other fashion. There is no special merit in being served first or any humiliation in being served last. At this table we are all equal, for we all come as sinners in need of the grace of God. No one is in danger of being left out. Everyone has a place at this table.

If you are a Christian, then consider your place at this table reserved, thanks to the gracious invitation of the One who hosts this gathering and welcomes us joyfully—Jesus Christ himself. And when we leave this table, it always should be with the recognition that there is still room at the table for more. Others can have a place here with us—if only they will answer the invitation of the Host.

Make it Your Own

Have you ever been present at a meal when the individuals or organization hosting the event ran out of food? Use that story to begin this meditation.

DATE USED _____

LITTLE THINGS MEAN A LOT

(SUITABLE FOR VALENTINE'S DAY)
ZECHARIAH 4:10

When I was in the ministry, I had the opportunity to conduct a number of weddings. During most ceremonies, a time was set aside for the exchanging of rings between the bride and groom. The minister's manual that I used to help arrange a wedding ceremony included these words that were to be spoken by the minister when the rings were exchanged:

Though small in size, these rings are large in significance. Made of precious metal, they remind us that love is not cheap nor common; indeed, love may cost us dearly. Made in a circle, their design tells us that love must never come to an end; we must keep it continuous. As you wear these rings, whether together or apart for a moment, may they be constant reminders of these glad promises you are making today.

(*Christian Minister's Manual,* Cincinnati: Standard Publishing Co., 1984.)

Yes, in spite of its size, a ring conveys significance to a husband and wife. If you've ever lost a wedding ring, think how frantic you became when you realized it was missing! Think of how relieved you felt when it turned up!

As is true with a wedding ring, the importance of the emblems of the Lord's Supper is not in their size. In fact, consider how the words quoted above could be altered somewhat and applied to the Supper.

Though small in size, these emblems are large in significance. Both of these emblems (the bread and the juice) were obtained at a price. Grains of wheat had to be crushed to make the bread; grapes had to be broken and crushed to make this juice. These emblems remind us that our salvation was purchased at a price far greater than what it costs to make bread or juice. God's love is not cheap or common; indeed, his love cost the life of his only Son. As we take these emblems now, may they remind us of the love that Jesus has for us, and of our responsibility to serve him faithfully, knowing that he died that we may live.

Make it Your Own

Have you ever lost a ring or something small that held great personal or sentimental value? Tell that story here.

96

DATE USED _____

THE GREAT EMANCIPATOR

(SUITABLE FOR PRESIDENT'S DAY) JOHN
8:31-36

Many of us recall learning about Abraham
Lincoln during elementary school. I can still
remember making a silhouette of Lincoln
(similar to the profile one sees on a penny)
using black paper, which we then pasted to
a white background and displayed around
the classroom, then eventually took home.

As I grew older and developed a greater
interest in American history, I began to
appreciate the simple, humble background
and character of Mr. Lincoln, which made
him an unlikely candidate for President of
the United States and yet continues to
endear him to so many of us—perhaps
because we long for that simplicity in the
political realm today.

Nowadays we combine Mr. Lincoln's and
George Washington's birthdays into one
President's Day. An unfortunate result of this
is that we don't really give Mr. Lincoln the
recognition he deserves. He was an outstanding leader of our nation at a critical
time in its history, and (as far as we can tell
from the available records) he was a man of
deep religious convictions.

Among his most notable achievements was the signing of a document called the Emancipation Proclamation, the beginning of which reads as follows: "That on the first day of January, in the year of our Lord one thousand eight hundred and sixty-three, all persons held as slaves within any State, or designated part of a State, . . . shall be then, thenceforward, and forever free."

When Jesus spoke the words, "You will know the truth, and the truth will set you free," he was issuing the everlasting Emancipation Proclamation. Immediately the Jews who heard him questioned his statement. "Why, we've never been slaves to anyone," they protested. "We don't need a deliverer." In the same way, many today object to the suggestion that they need Jesus, blind to the fact that they are actually in bondage to the cruelest, most hideous form of slavery known to man—the slavery of sin.

As we gather before this Communion table, we come to honor the Savior who died and rose again that we who were slaves to sin may be truly emancipated— "then, thenceforward, and forever free."

DATE USED _____

Make it Your Own

Do you know a story about Abraham Lincoln, or recall one that you learned in school? Use that story to introduce this meditation.

98

A MOTHER'S LOVE

What do you think of when you think of a mother's love? What specific act comes to mind? It may well be something having to do with a mother's special ability to care for her children during a time of pain or illness. Perhaps you're thinking of a mother rocking a fretful baby, or pressing her face against a child's forehead to see if there's any fever, or wiping the tears from a child's face after a fall outside.

When I was a child I had frequent earaches, especially during the winter months. Many were the times that my mother would stay beside me through the night. She would usually get a washcloth, heat it over the stove, then place it on my ear to relieve the pain so I could go to sleep. I've seen my wife show the same kind of care for our three children—putting their welfare ahead of hers.

John is the only Gospel writer who tells of Jesus' care for his mother while he was dying on the cross. Think of it: Jesus was giving his life for the sins of the world and of all of human history, bearing the guilt of those millions of people—yet took the time to care for the well-being of his mother.

What do you suppose Mary was thinking while all this was happening? Here was the baby she once carried in her womb, the toddler she watched as he took his first steps, the boy who probably helped his earthly father Joseph in the carpenter's shop. Now he hung before her—suffering, bleeding, in indescribable agony. She must have wanted to do something—anything—motherly to relieve her son's pain.

Yet all the Scripture says is, "Near the cross of Jesus stood his mother" (John 19:25). She stood, for there was *nothing* she could do. As unbelievable as it may seem, there is a love stronger than even a mother's love; and Mary appeared to realize that. Jesus was not only Mary's son; he was God's Son. That day at Calvary the love of God for a lost world overruled the love of a mother for her hurting son.

The love of God is the message of these emblems. It is a love that has made it possible for us to enjoy the blessing and the companionship of our mothers not only on this earth but in the higher, grander joys of Heaven.

Make it Your Own

Do you have a special memory of how your mother helped you when you hurt yourself or were ill? Tell that story to introduce this meditation.

DATE USED _____

PROUD FATHER

(SUITABLE FOR FATHER'S DAY)
HEBREWS 2:10-13

As a father, I've watched our children's involvement in numerous activities, and witnessed various milestones. Different highlights come to mind: our daughter's graduation from high school, our older son recording a sack at a high-school football game, our younger son pitching for his Little League team. I've also been privileged to watch each child being baptized into Christ and to baptize our two boys.

To witness such moments as these makes any father or mother grateful to God for the privilege of parenthood. One is led to think back to the days when the children would first learn to ride a bike, color a picture, or tie a shoe, and would shout with excitement, "Look at me, Daddy!" And you have to keep looking (even when they would prefer you didn't)—or you'll miss so much.

As we take the Lord's Supper today and as we look at the emblems representing Jesus' body and blood, let's try to think about what it was like for God the Father to look at his Son's real body and blood and to see him treated so unfairly at Calvary. How anguished the Father's heart must have been to hear his Son cry, "My God, my God, why have you forsaken me?" (Matthew 27:46). And yet, during those hours on the cross, Jesus was doing his Father's bidding. He could say, "I have brought you glory on earth by completing the work you gave me to do" (John 17:4). Though the Father's words, "This is my Son, whom I love; with him I am well pleased," were not uttered at the crucifixion, they surely could have been. Jesus' enemies thought that his death was a sign that God had forsaken him (Matthew 27:43). But they were wrong. This was a Father's proud moment.

Hebrews 2:10 tells us that one of the results of the Son's death was to bring "many sons to glory." Thus he can declare, "Here am I, and the children God has given me" (v. 13). On this Lord's Day, the Father looks down upon assemblies such as ours and rejoices in his fellowship with members of his family all across the globe. This too is a Father's proud moment.

Proverbs 10:1 tells us, "A wise son brings joy to his father." As we take these emblems, let us resolve to so live that we will bring joy —and many proud moments—to our Father.

Make it Your Own

Can you think of something that one of your children (or a child in your extended family) did that made you especially proud of him or her? Use that story to begin this meditation.

DATE USED _____

IN GOOD HANDS

(SUITABLE FOR LABOR DAY)
JOHN 20:19, 20, 26-28

While preparing this meditation, I began to think about the part hands had played and would play in the production of the book in which it would be included. I wrote (and sometimes rewrote, rewrote, and rewrote!) each meditation on a piece of scrap paper. Next I typed the material on a computer. Then I handed the manuscript to the editor. At that point, other hands took over the publication process: hands that set type, hands that operated presses and binders, hands that packed, distributed, and displayed, and now *your* hands are holding the finished product!

This is Labor Day weekend—a good time to think about the use of our hands. Just think of all we do every day that requires the use of our hands! Where would we be without them? How much could we accomplish without our hands?

Jesus used his hands as we do, to work, to dress, to eat. His hands—and ours—have wiped away tears and comforted the lonely. But Jesus was able to use his hands in ways that we cannot—to heal the sick, to make the blind see, and to bless little children.

Think about the many ways that Jesus used his hands as he carried out the work his heavenly Father had given him to do.

Yet it was in his death, as he hung with hands nailed to the cross, that Jesus accomplished his most important work. Think of how those hands were pierced with nails when Jesus was crucified. The hands that had brought joy to so many lives and had done nothing but good for others were treated as though they were the hands of a criminal. His work that day was to end spiritual blindness and bring spiritual healing. And we remember his ultimate "labor of love" whenever we take the Lord's Supper.

Make it Your Own

Do you know a story that you could tell about the importance of hands (perhaps one from your workplace)? Use that story to begin this meditation.

Have you ever thought about how we take these emblems? We use our *hands* to bring the bread to our mouths and the cup to our lips. Today as you partake, think not only about the meaning of the emblems, but also about the hands that you use to hold them. Think about the hands of Jesus nailed to a cross for you. Think of him standing before you, as he stood before doubting Thomas, and saying, "See my hands." And think of yourself presenting your hands in loving service to Jesus.

DATE USED _____

THE FAMILY DINNER

(SUITABLE FOR THANKSGIVING)
MATTHEW 4:4; JOHN 6:35

For me, going home for Thanksgiving always has been a very special tradition, made especially so by the opportunity it gives my family to be together. The highlight of the day is an afternoon meal at which we enjoy an abundance of good things to eat, topped off by an assortment of great desserts—though usually dessert has to wait a little while because we've eaten so much during the meal! The rest of the day is spent watching football, playing family games, and somehow finding time (and room!) enough for an evening meal.

It is easy to take for granted such happy times, delicious food, and wonderful company. Those of us who experience them should never forget what blessings these are and how many homes at Thanksgiving are without them. We are indeed wealthy.

This Communion table is not distinguished by the wide variety of foods one sees on it. It really presents quite a contrast to the tables to which most of us sit down at Thanksgiving. Here there is no smorgasbord. The fare is simple: bread and juice. That is because the real hunger being addressed here is not of the stomach; it is of the soul. There is not a variety of items from which to choose at this table, because we have made our most important choice already: to live by faith, not by sight, and to make eternal matters a higher priority than temporal matters. We acknowledge that "man does not live on bread alone, but on every word that comes from the mouth of God" (Matthew 4:4).

In addition, we are gathered at this table with family—those "born not of natural descent, nor of human decision or a husband's will, but born of God" (John 1:13). Despite our different earthly parents, we have a common heavenly Father. Despite our different places of birth, we have a common destination—Heaven. Despite the different goals that we pursue, we have one overriding aim: to be Christ's people every day in every circumstance.

Here at this table we experience a different kind of fullness—a satisfaction that the world cannot provide. As Jesus said, "I am the bread of life. He who comes to me will never go hungry, and he who believes in me will never be thirsty" (John 6:35). For all that this table represents, let us give thanks.

DATE USED _____

Make it Your Own

Can you tell about a memorable Thanksgiving dinner or a Thanksgiving tradition that involved or currently involves your family? Use that story at the beginning of this meditation.

106

WHERE ARE THEY NOW?

(SUITABLE FOR CHRISTMAS)
MATTHEW 1:18-21

When the church that our family attends celebrated its fiftieth anniversary, a special Sunday of activities was planned to mark the milestone. Two of the former ministers of the congregation were invited to return and speak, and invitations were sent out to as many former members as we could possibly obtain addresses for. Pictures that highlighted key events in the history of the church were compiled and posted for people to see. The day was filled with glimpses into the past and challenges to fill the next fifty years with many more precious memories in the service of the Lord.

Whenever people try to get a group together for a special occasion the questions are asked, "Where is he now?" "What has happened to this person?" Some searches reap happy rewards; others uncover sad news.

During this special occasion called Christmas, the tendency is to focus on Jesus as a baby in Bethlehem's manger—gentle, innocent, harmless. And all too many want to leave him in that very spot, never realizing, or perhaps unwilling (even afraid) to acknowledge, that Bethlehem was just the beginning of the record of the One called Immanuel ("God with us").

What happened to him? Where is he now? This Communion table reminds us of the purpose for which this baby was born—to grow to adulthood and become the Lamb of God who would take away the sins of the world (John 1:29). This is the purpose to which the angel alluded when he spoke to Joseph in a dream to allay his fears regarding Mary: he would "save his people from their sins" (Matthew 1:21). The events *after* Bethlehem constitute the real message of Christmas. And that includes Jesus' promise that he will come again to take his people to be with him forever—a truth that this table also calls us to keep in mind (1 Corinthians 11:26).

Yes, Bethlehem was just the beginning. To know and understand "the rest of the story" (as Paul Harvey puts it) is to know and understand the meaning of Christmas.

Make it Your Own

Have you ever been involved in planning a special event (such as a reunion or anniversary of some kind) that involved attempting to answer the question, "Where are they now"? Did you find out something surprising or unusual? Use that story to begin this meditation.

DATE USED _____

A Father's Lullaby

(Suitable for Christmas)
Matthew 1:18-21

We often think of Mother as the parent who lovingly sang lullabies to us. Some of us have equally fond memories of Mother rocking and gently singing to a younger brother or sister. To see her performing the same role years later as a grandmother to our children brings a feeling of genuine contentment. I've also had the privilege of seeing my wife rocking our children to sleep (though the running joke in our family was that the rocking put her to sleep faster than the kids!).

Many writers have pictured Mary, the mother of Jesus, gently speaking or singing to Jesus. Some years ago I read a poem that looked at this scenario from a very different and heartwarming perspective. It is entitled "Joseph's Lullaby."

Sleep now, little one.
I will watch while you and your mother sleep.
I wish I could do more.
This straw is not good enough for you.
Back in Nazareth I'll make a proper bed for you
of seasoned wood, smooth, strong, well-pegged.
A bed fit for a carpenter's son.

Just wait till we get back to Nazareth.
I'll teach you everything I know.
You'll learn to choose the cedar wood, eucalyptus
    and fir.
You'll learn to use the drawshave, ax and saw.
Your arms will grow strong, your hands rough—
    like these.
You will bear the pungent smell of new wood
and wear shavings and sawdust in your hair.

You'll be a man whose life centers
on hammer and nails and wood.
But for now,
sleep, little Jesus, sleep.
(*Decision*, December 1973.)

Yes, Jesus' life did center on hammer, nails, and wood—not because he came to be a carpenter, but because he came to be a Savior. In this season, we honor not only the Christ of the manger, but the Christ of the cross. For at the cross he fulfilled the angel's words spoken to Joseph: "he will save his people from their sins."

Make it Your Own

Do you have a memory or a story about a lullaby that someone in your family liked (or likes) to sing? Use that story to introduce this meditation.

DATE USED _____

INDEX OF SCRIPTURES